STORIES WE LIVE
CUENTOS QUE VIVIMOS

The Madeleva Lecture in Spirituality

This series, sponsored by the Center for Spirituality, Saint Mary's College, Notre Dame, Indiana, honors annually the woman who as president of the college inaugurated its pioneering graduate program in theology, Sister M. Madeleva, C.S.C.

STORIES WE LIVE
CUENTOS QUE VIVIMOS

Hispanic Women's Spirituality

JEANETTE RODRIGUEZ

1996 Madeleva Lecture
in Spirituality

PAULIST PRESS
New York/Mahwah, N.J.

The poem by R. Castro appears by permission of its author.

Cover by Morris Berman Studio.

The painting, *Las Madrecitas,* by Cecilia Alvarez is used with permission of Concilio for the Spanish Speaking.

ISBN: 0-8091-3659-7

Published by Paulist Press
997 Macarthur Boulevard
Mahwah, NJ 07430

Printed and bound in the
United States of America

Dedication

For my sisters Sylvia and Linda
and my comadre Cristina.
Their strength, wisdom and
great stories have continued
to nurture and accompany
me in La Vida.

Jeanette Rodriguez, Ph.D. presently teaches systematic theology at Seattle University. She received an MA (1978) from Fordham University, an MA (1981) from the University of Guam, and her Ph.D. (1990) from the Graduate Theological Union, Berkeley. Her areas of interest and expertise are theological anthropology, U.S. Hispanic theology, the theologies of liberation and Hispanic women's spirituality. She is a board member of the Academy of Hispanic Theologians of the U.S. (ACHTUS) and an editorial board member of the *Journal of Hispanic/Catholic Theology*. Her publications include *Our Lady of Guadalupe*, published by the University of Texas Press.

HISPANIC WOMEN'S STORIES OF STRUGGLE, WISDOM AND SURVIVAL

INTRODUCTION

Let me begin by thanking all those involved for inviting me to present the Madeleva Lecture in Spirituality for 1996. I am always pleased to have an opportunity to share with you my reflections regarding theology and Hispanic women's spirituality. I'd like to outline briefly what I hope to do in this lecture. First, I'd like to say a few words about tradition, specifically about one source of tradition which is stories. Second, I'd like to share with you an original notion of cultural memory and third, share the concrete stories of Hispanic/Latina women struggling to understand their life and to live life with dignity, integrity, and love.

Theology is faith trying to express itself. In theology we give expression to what we already know. It especially articulates the language of faith and refers to an experience of living. In this context I am seeking to articulate faith reflections on the struggles of Hispanic/Latina women with a particular focus on spirituality. One of the many contributions I have received from Third World feminist theologians is an understanding of theology that has to do with the word "life." In all continents, "women are deeply committed to life, giving life, and protecting life...Third World theologians find themselves committed and faithful to all the vital elements that compose human life. Their theologizing is deeply rooted in experience, in affection, in life."[1]

Ann Carr contends that spirituality encompasses all of our relationships. Carr contends that spirituality encompasses our relationships to all of creation. This is inclusive of not just our social network, family, work, recreation, but nature itself. I like her claim that spirituality is larger than a theology because it is all-encompassing. She further acknowledges that spirituality is "deeply formed by family, teachers, friends, community, class, race, culture, sex, and by our time in history, just as it is influenced by beliefs, intellectual position and moral options. These influences may be unconscious or made explicit...and while being individually patterned it is culturally shaped."[2]

Both African and Latin American theologians explain that their way to a theological reformulation is firmly and deeply planted in human life, where they believe the Holy Spirit lives and acts.

In my doctoral studies at Berkeley I was taught that theology is a discipline that exists specifically to articulate the language of faith. Though I also believe that theology starts from experience and reflects God's self-communication in the history of the world, I have discovered also that there is a way of doing theology that starts with shared experiences from oral transmission, "for the simple fact of sharing life." Brazilian theologian Ivone Gebara writes:

> Many women are specially gifted with a deep intuition about human life and are able to counsel, to intuit problems, to express them, to give support, to propose solutions, and to confirm the faith of many people...This activity springs from life and life is its reference point. It is received as a gift from God and handed on as a gift. Thus discourse dealing with the important issues in life is the heart of every theology.[3]

Because theology is what happens when faith tries to express itself, theology will always be inadequate since faith deals with realities that cannot be fully or properly expressed. The other distinction, which I think is important to highlight, is that whereas our faith is one and unchanging in kind, theology is plural. It is changing and culturally conditioned. Whenever I engage in theology I find three questions particularly helpful: 1) Under what conditions is this theology being done? 2) For whom is theology done? 3) To whom is it addressed? With the emergence of liberation theology, and specifically women doing theology, we are no longer willing to wait for others to define or validate our experience of life and faith. Women and those who are in a constant state of oppression have decided to define themselves. They want to express in their own words their particular way of experiencing God and their particular way of living their faith. In the midst of a reality in which women are doubly or triply oppressed, doing liberation theology from a woman's perspective is not a luxury, but a necessity and a right to be claimed.

One may ask, how do women's claims about their experience extend beyond critique to construct proposals about rethinking, reimagining, and revisioning our tradition? Theologian Sue Secker believes that the reason women are insisting upon the truth in their experience is that theirs is of a fundamental "contrast experience" that happens as they do theology. Once we are confronted with the absence of our perspective and our voices in the Christian theological tradition, contends Secker, we cannot but insist with theologian Rosemary Radford Reuther that whatever denies, diminishes, or distorts the full humanity of women is not redemptive.

In an attempt to respond to this non-redemptive condition of the dearth of knowledge about Hispanic women's spirituality, or the limited amount written about Hispanic women's spirituality, I have dedicated most of my writing to the discovery and articulation of what is important to Hispanic women. Needless to say this approach is always problematic because of the diversity of the Hispanic population. And once again, under what conditions are we doing theology? Are we doing it with highly articulated, highly educated, acculturated, monolingual, English-speaking persons? Or are we dealing with lower-level educated, monolingual Spanish-speaking recent immigrants? Depending on which Hispanics we are dealing with, each and every cluster has a contribution to make to the theological enterprise. The power to name one's experience, one's identity, is crucial. The Spanish word *experiencia* is not used the same way as "experience" is used in English. When we want to discuss our experience in Spanish, we talk about *la realidad*, our lived experiences.

I am North American and Hispanic, that is, U.S. born of Ecuadorian parents. This special circumstance endows my existence, my very reality, with conflict.

As a U.S. Hispanic theologian, my identity at times is conflictual and tense because of another double identity, that of a university professor on the one hand, and a U.S. Hispanic on the other. My primary identity is given to me by my people, the Hispanic communities of the U.S., whom I seek to accompany. Intrinsic to this process of accompaniment is a process of critical discernment.

Those of us who are committed to solidarity are often accused of not being academic or scholarly enough. But I believe that those of us involved in this kind of theology that take seriously the integration of theory and practice are in the process of redefining scholarship itself. Our task is not to give up reason or skill development in favor of cultural affection, but to demonstrate that scholarship in theology must take seriously the context of theology. This shift in theological adequacy includes both rational and affective expressions of faith, with a careful eye to the justice needs of the vast majority of humanity.[4]

Starting from a position of the unknown, I have sought to throw out my theological net in an attempt to identify what may in fact be important to Latina women; and therefore to learn something about what we as theologians should be thinking, reflecting, or dialoging about. Given this position, I have chosen to focus on women's stories. I believe that we tell stories about ourselves and about our lives to feel more connected. Stories connect us with the past, they help us to understand the present, they offer hope about the future. In any case stories can scare us, shame us, and/or delight us. They can provide a source of calmness when we are overwhelmed; they may mend our broken hearts; they may reveal new perspectives. Stories can entertain, instruct, and serve as bridges in order to establish new relationships. Stories invite the "other" into our own process of theological reflection: hence the quality of conversation deepens.

THE TASK

In hopes of tapping *living stories*, stories we live, I decided to ask the following question of Latina women: What story were you told by your mother, your grandmother, your comadre (co-mother, godmother of child), tia (aunt) that you will never forget? A story that had a significant impact on you, taught you something, and is a story that you carry with you for the rest of your life? Needless to say, this was a difficult question because the Latina culture is a culture of storytelling. There are numerous stories that many of us have been raised on. What I sought, however, was that one story that each of the women would never forget. If there is a story that you cannot forget, it is usually a story that you will pass on. I collected more than one hundred stories. I wanted to collect enough so that I could discover if a kind of theological construct would emerge. As you will see, what emerged was more revelatory than I could have imagined.

Before I share those stories I would like to outline for you an understanding of story as a method for transmitting what I term cultural memory.

Cultural Memory/Tradition

In many ways cultural memory can be likened to tradition in that tradition passes on a world of meaning from generation to generation. Tradition, as well as cultural memory, carries all these experiences, personal as well as communal, to the people. Implicit and explicit understandings, myths, stories, affect anything that actualizes the potential of the human person. Charles Davis notes:

> A tradition is a way of responding to reality including feelings, memories, images, ideas, attitudes, interpersonal relationships; in brief, the entire complex that forms life within a particular world, a world bonded by a horizon that determines the particular sense of reality that pervades it.[5]

Tradition has two distinct parts: the process, the actual handing on of tradition, and the *traditium*, the content and product. In other words, tradition could be both a participle (remembering), and a noun (a memory). The participle and noun are two sides of the same coin. Cultural memory has the same two elements attributed to tradition. It is both remembering and a memory. Cultural memory is remembering, tradition, the process. Who remembers? A people within a culture. An individual within a group. It is the people or the individuals that carry a memory. How is it remembered? Memory, oral and written accounts, celebrations, sacred space—all contribute to cultural remembering. What *traditium* is being remembered? What does this memory do? What does it evoke? What are its manifestations?

Cultural memories are manifested in affectivity, ideas, aspirations, beliefs, stories. In my book *Our Lady Guadalupe: Faith and Empowerment among Mexican-American Women*, I identified Our Lady of Guadalupe as a cultural memory. The memory of Our Lady of Guadalupe is carried and transmitted in the stories Latina women share and by the devotions that express faith in her. Cultural memory is contained in the image of Guadalupe itself; it is recorded in the Aztec document entitled "Nican Mopohua." In the celebrations on Our Lady's feast in December, Guadalupe is made present. The remembering and evoking is mainly a matter of feelings and aspirations, of searching for hope and strength. A memory, like Guadalupe, is carried by a people in their historical, social, and political world. In a culture, a social group consciously and unconsciously passes along value-laden memories. This memory of Our Lady of Guadalupe passes on the value of self-worth, of appreciation of one's own culture and tradition. The image and message of Our Lady of Guadalupe, therefore, are vehicles for cultural memory. As cultural memory, Guadalupe evokes an affectivity that bonds individuals not only to her but to each other, thus becoming a key element in their sense of being a community of people.

Cultural memory bears similarities to both historical memory and myth. Like historical memory, cultural memory is rooted in actual events and in the surrounding and resulting alignment of images, symbols, and affectivity which are even more pervasive than "facts." Many kinds of historical memories are transmitted through text, oral history, tradition, plays, personal and collective memory. Occasionally, historical memories are so overwhelmingly important that they define the essence of a people and are imperative to their survival. An implied distinction could be highlighted here. "Historical memory" tends to be constructed to support those in power. Cultural memory can either support the dominant culture or, as with Guadalupe, subvert it by empowering the marginalized cultures.

Unlike myth, cultural memory has a historical basis; however, like myth, it can be transformative. It has power to influence human life. Wendy O'Flaherty tells us:

> A myth is a story that is sacred to and shared by a group of people who find their most important meanings in it; it is a story believed to have been composed in the past about an event in the past...an event that continues to have meaning in the present because it is remembered; it is a story that is part of a larger group of stories.[6]

The transforming characteristic attributed to myth is also characteristic of the process of cultural memory. **Cultural memory transmits an experience rooted in history that has reached a culturally definitive transformative status.** The myth/story of Guadalupe is a cultural memory because it "enshrines the major hopes and aspirations of an entire society."[7]

Cultural memory does not necessarily originate from a calamity, but most often it does arise out of events that are transformative, that bring about recognizable shifts in the world of meaning of a people. Cultural memory fulfills the need to transcend certain events or circumstances (the Jewish people and the Holocaust) and/or to maintain a corporate identity such as an historical event used to create patriotism (the American Patriots and the Boston Tea Party; Mexican identity and Guadalupe). This memory passes from generation to generation, from parent to child, from leader to follower, through oral traditions, written accounts, images, rituals, and drama. Cultural memory is evoked around image, symbol, affect, or event precisely because it keeps alive and transforms those events of the past, which continue to give meaning to the present.

The Guadalupe event is rooted in history. It has a given content. Like all memories, cultural memory changes over time. Culture is a living and dynamic reality. Memory contributes to the defining and redefining of a given culture. This holding on to, passing on and reinterpreting the memory is both an intellectual and affective process.

What theological insights can be gathered from the cultural memory of Our Lady of Guadalupe? First, from a theological perspective, memory serves as an "expression of eschatological hope" and a "category of the salvation of identity."[8] Johann Baptist Metz takes this approach in his fundamental theology, where he states that memory, especially as "the memory of suffering" is the basic concept in a theological theory of history and society.[9] Metz argues that "memory can have a very decisive ecclesiological importance in defining the Church as a public vehicle transmitting a dangerous memory in a system of social life."[10] Guadalupe represents an eschatological hope for those who believe in her. Guadalupe reminds us that the way the world is, is not the way it was meant to be. Therefore, to uphold the memory of the Guadalupe event shows "solidarity in memory with the dead and the conquered."[11] The dead and the conquered Nahautl people, Latina women, all oppressed and marginalized people, may be resurrected in the Guadalupe event. The Guadalupe event reminds us that the manifestation of the divine takes her stand with the marginalized and oppressed and shows them love, compassion, help, and defense. The Guadalupe event, memory, story, recalls who we are as a people, how we have been oppressed, and how God sides with the poor and calls us all to liberation and healing.

The cultural memory of the Guadalupe event exists because there is a need for it to exist. Succinctly, Guadalupe as cultural memory continues to exist because it feeds a basic need for identity, salvation, hope and resistance to annihilation. The Guadalupe story speaks of the restoration of human dignity in a voice once silenced and now restored. It speaks of the restoration of a lost language and a way of perceiving the divine. It speaks of assessing lost symbols and transforming them in a new time. Ultimately, it speaks and continues to speak of a shared experience of a people—a people that suffers.

God is faithful to the covenant promise that God is *our* God and we are God's people.

Guadalupe is a manifestation of this biblical covenant. Metz states that

> Christian faith can be understood as an attitude according to which man remembers promises that have been made and hopes that are experienced as a result of those promises and commits himself to those memories.[12]

This is what a devotee of Guadalupe does. The devotee, through cultural memory, remembers the promises of compassion, help and defense that Guadalupe initially made. These promises are experienced by the people as hope, a hope carried in and expressed through cultural memory, retelling the story, celebrating the feast, visiting the Basilica, praying before the Virgin's image, and working for justice. As a result of these promises the devotee is committed to the Guadalupan memory and image, that which can be read, touched, felt, seen, experienced. What other memories, images, insights have been transmitted consciously or unconsciously?

In the next section we will examine the daily stories transmitted from woman to woman as a potential source of guidance, hope, and warning.

It is my perspective that personal experience serves as a critical basis for knowledge and skill acquisition. When this is done in a shared context where one's testimony through story is given, it can play a very powerful role for women. It affirms and enhances their sharing of life.

There is still so little we understand about Hispanic women's spirituality. On a hunch I sought to collect stories that were significant to the women with whom I spoke. In an attempt to unearth what was important to them, I asked an open-ended question rather than setting my own agenda.

As I mentioned above, I decided to ask Hispanic/Latina women from a variety of Hispanic ethnic backgrounds to remember a story that was significant to them. It would have to be a story that their mother or their grandmother told them. The story had to be passed on by a woman. Our culture is a culture of stories, so it was a very hard question for people to answer. Because ours is a culture of stories, there was difficulty in making a distinction between consejos (advice giving) and proverbs and stories.

I did not want to define the categories rigidly for fear of losing pearls of wisdom. All I wanted to know was the things they had heard their mother, their grandmother, or aunt say; what they remembered; what story had had some kind of effect on them. This was the story that I sought. I wanted those stories that continue to live in their lives.

I began the interviewing process by sharing a story that my mother had told me. When I was in junior high, my sister got into a fight and I said some awful things to her. My mother pulled me aside and said, "You really need to be careful what you say because words are like feathers in a pillow. Your words are like the woman who climbed to the top of the mountain and let all the feathers out—you can never gather them together again." And that's all she said to me. Somehow, I understood. And so I invite you to be open to the wisdom, the pain, and the truths that emerge from the following stories.

Cecilia (Mexican-American), 41 years old

Well the first story that she (mother) told me was I guess her way of passing on her experiences as a young girl, giving me a sense of history.

The story that she told me had to do with World War II and what she described was the neighborhood in which she lived. The homes were close together and everyone knew each other. It was a very close, tight-knit community. After all, almost all, really all, were Chicanos. And the story goes like this...in the middle of

the night, during World War II, you know very late at night, it was one of the most fearful times of night for that community because basically what happened was that sometime during the middle of the night they would hear this bell. It was the bell of a messenger coming to deliver a letter to a family there in that community. And the letter was from the military letting them know that they had lost a son, a father, or a husband in the war.

The way my mother told the story made it seem like it always happened very late at night, in the dead of night, when everyone was asleep. So the sound of the bell was unmistakable. And what would happen is that people would wake up when they would hear that bell. Most everyone had a son in that war; every household was waiting for the sound of the bell to stop in front of their home. And what my mom would describe was that as the bell traveled down the street the lights would go on for people waiting to see where it was going to stop. And, as it passed your house there was always a sense of relief in that household but eventually the bell would stop and there would be this dead quiet and then the next sound that you would hear would be this wail. You know, coming from someone's home. You know, she would tell the

story to me and it never failed to evoke emotion in me and in her.

At this point in the interview I made the observation to Cecilia that it was obvious that the retelling of the story was evoking a great deal of emotion and what was that about? She answered, "It's just the sadness of the kind of pain a family experiences when they lose somebody. I've never been in my mother's shoes, but for some reason when she'd tell the story I'd identify with it. My mother would cry. Part of the story for my mother was that her brother was in Germany at the time and they were very fortunate because they never lost anyone. But still, my mother would cry when she would tell me the story and I'd start to cry. I don't know, maybe it was because I was a little girl." In which case I responded, "But you're not a little girl now and you're crying."

Cecilia responds, "I think the emotion I feel says something about how I experience history. I experience history through my mother. You know in that particular story somehow I feel like I knew the 1930's and 1940's because my mother and I would spend a lot of time talking about the old days, what it was like when she was young. And I think in doing this she passed on a sense of how hard it was for her and how she wanted advantages for me. I think that was always the most explicit thing in her story. It was to give me a sense of some of the things she had gone through in the hopes that I would learn something from it, and be very interested in what it was like, you know back then in history."

Many of these interviews were conducted with groups of women. Cecilia shared her story and in response her friend wrote the following poem:

Abuela's Story Remembered

She told me the story
of a barrio
on a few blocks of street
between St. Henry's and the underpass
almost in the shadows
Sonora Street Southside San Antonio

"It was during World War II, mijita
when almost every family
prayed for silence
But near midnight
the bicycled messenger's bell
lit each light on the block.
A knock and then the childbirth cry recalled.

We took what was at hand as offerings
whispered prayers
and spoke soft memories only mothers can bear.
On the nights of the bicycled messenger's bell

we clung one to the other, stilled our breathing
knowing in a moment the world ends a second
  time.

Each one here lost another.

¿Did I tell you mijita que pequeño era mi barrio?"
R. Castro

The spirituality that emerges from this story
and its pregnant images of night, bell, lights, whispered prayers, indicates how one copes with life
and death and how life and death is dealt with
here in community. When the messenger's bell
rings all the lights go on, not only the lights of the
person receiving the message. The community is
in tune—aware of the impending tragedy—a witness to sorrow as experienced in the wail.

Some people say that faith has to do with how
we interpret these places in our lives where we
run up against limits. In this story and the stories
that follow these women are crashing into their
limits all the time. They crash into their pain, suffering, loss, death, the silence, the shadows, all
the different words that are used here. This is
their faith story. And what happens when they
crash into these things? Do they give up? Do they
go away in despair? No! They go on living. They
go on coping. They go on doing what has to be
done. How do they do it? They are inspired; they

are full of grace. They do it in community, they do it together. It seems to me that the lesson for us is to ask: How important is it for us to be conscious and intentional about the way we talk about life? These women are not conscious and intentional about God. They are very intentional about life. And yet if it is true, as the New Testament states, that God is life, then they are in the very source of life.

WISDOM STORIES: THE KINGDOM OF GOD IS LIKE...

Jesus' verbal gifts were incredible. He spoke in a poetic and imaginative way, and his speech was filled with provocative statements. He was a teacher of wisdom using "the classic forms of wisdom speech (parables, and memorable short sayings known as aphorisms) to teach a subversive and alternative wisdom."[13] I am indebted to Marcus Borg's understanding of Jesus as a teacher of wisdom, and to the distinction he makes between conventional wisdom and what he calls alternative wisdom. We focus here on conventional wisdom because the stories you are about to read from these Hispanic Latina women, I believe, fall under this particular kind of wisdom. Conventional wisdom captures the worldview or image of reality of a given culture. It is talking about a way to live; it is an anchor, if you will. It provides guidance about how to live. It can range from practical etiquette images to what constitutes a proper and good life within the culture. "Conventional wisdom embodies the essential value of a culture."[14]

The following are examples of conventional wisdom shared by the Latina women I interviewed. Wisdom is a wonderful feminine image so it seems appropriate that these women carry forward the wisdom tradition.

Mari (Mexican American), 74 years old

My mother always said that we (children) were her little trees that she had to constantly guide so that we would grow up straight and not chueco (crooked). Once I got in trouble in school for fighting with another girl because she made fun of my name and my mother sat me down and told me that if I followed those actions I would end up being a crooked little tree.

Christina (Mexican American), 11 years old

When I was a little girl my mother always told me the story of Diocito when we were in church. I loved her telling me this story and when she was done I would ask her to tell me over and over again. She had make me love him. I realized later that part of the reason she always told me the story in church was to keep me quiet. It doesn't matter; I still remember it and I still enjoy that she did that.

Sylvia (Mexican American), 15 years old

My mother always tells me that in me I carry the blood of very proud and strong women and that I have a responsibility to develop these qualities in myself. I have the security of throwing on restraint when I need it. My mother says that my great grandmother Santos' spirit is always around for guidance and comfort. She tells me that all the pride and strength will shine through me for other people to see and use as an example. She says we all make mistakes in life because these are the lessons that develop our character. She says that if we were born knowing everything we might as well be dead. She says that there is no shame in making mistakes but it is foolish not to learn from them. She also says that there is nothing in the world that would stop her from loving us. We could commit the most horrible acts and she would still love us. She wouldn't like what we did but her love will last even after she is dead.

Sylvia appears to have received a spirituality that invites her to grow, to risk knowing that "failure" can be a learning moment. Risk does not need to be feared. She is invited to see life more creatively, with freedom to discover more fully the woman that she truly is to become. Her story invites us to look at our own attitudes towards risk, failure, growth, and in so doing, move outside ourselves into Sylvia's wisdom.

Beatrix (Mexican American), 50 years old

When I was growing up there was a lot of pressure about being feminine like my older sister. I was dressed up in silly things for parties and constantly asked what boy I liked. I didn't want to play house; I wanted to play army and I wanted to play general. When I became a teenager my mother could see how miserable I was becoming. She realized that I was being pushed by everyone including herself to be someone I was not. She sat me down and apologized for not seeing the qualities I already possessed rather than trying to change my personality into her dream of a daughter. She told me to continue developing my assertive nature and that from now on she would appreciate who I was. That was a very important day in my life. I went out to tackle all those challenges I always wanted to undertake, except now I knew I had the unconditional support of my mom behind me. Today my mother is a wonderful grandmother to all three of my daughters, even the one who says she always wanted to be a general.

Here we can feel Beatrix's pain and her mother's movement towards giving her freedom and acceptance. We discover a story about unconditional love and acceptance and a reminder of First Corinthians 12 that acknowledges the different gifts and talents that we, the human family, bring to one another.

Teresa (Cubana), 54 years old

I grew up in Havana, Cuba in a wealthy household. I was very close to my parents and my aunt. My parents ran a successful business. My aunt was my daily companion. She was a mathematician at the university. She never married. When Fidel came into power I was seventeen years old and had been a strong supporter of his with all my other idealistic friends. After about two months of Castro being in power, my mother knew the direction that Cuba was going in, so she arranged for me to travel to the United States. She was afraid for me. At the end of my second week in Florida, I received a phone call from my mother telling me that I was to stay in Florida until she could join me. I was devastated but my mother told me I had no choice but to be strong. Weakness was not an option. She explained that we had been very fortunate but life never runs on a smooth course. Now is when I would develop my strength as a person. She told me that she was always with me even though we were in different countries. I didn't like her words but I believed them and so I adjusted. Within one year I was sent to Chicago in the dead of winter. Within two more years my aunt was able to join me in Chicago. My mother finally joined us in California *thirteen years later*. It was very difficult to leave Cuba. Everything of our family's was confiscated by the government years ago and my mother was allowed to leave with her clothes, her wedding ring and one pair of earrings. Our life has not been easy, but gifts of courage and strength were given to me by my mother and my aunt. These are the riches in my life.

Marisol (Mexican American), 72 years old

My mother was quite a humble lady and we were very poor. My father had trouble keeping a job because it was very hard times. We went to church every Sunday and had a small altar in our house where my mother would pray every night. My father was not nice to my mother. And he often made her feel ignorant. I knew she wasn't but we were all afraid of my father. As I grew older and became a teenager I became more upset with my mother for not standing up to my father. I felt like I didn't respect her as much. One night I woke up because I heard a noise from the kitchen. I got up quietly to see what it was. My mother was kneeling down saying her prayers but this time she was crying. I heard her asking God not to let me hate her for not being stronger. She asked God to help me grow up to be stronger than she was. She told God how important it was for me to have a good life, feeling like I was worth something. She said she didn't want her children to grow up without a father because those children were treated like they were less. It was at this time I realized how much my mother had suffered because of her children. She gave up her own happiness for her children. This takes a lot of love. From that day on my mother was like a queen in my eyes. I became a strong person because I knew that was what she wanted for me.

We are invited into Marisol's moment of conversion. She embodies her mother's love and strength and perhaps challenges us to see our mother in a new light. Hers is a spirituality that is deeply incarnational.

Dolores (El Salvador), 35 years old

I left El Salvador when I was fifteen because I could not stand the brutality that I saw. I felt as if I would go crazy if I saw any more killing and atrocities. When I left my family I was very angry with God and told my mother right before I left that I no longer believed in her God. I told her that her God did not exist, that she only believed it because life was so horrible that she had to have some way of escaping. She told me that when I grew older I would realize that this was not God's work, it was the work of man. She said that ugliness all around did not mean that beauty did not and would not exist. She said we create beauty or ugliness because God gave us the choice. She asked me not to let an ugly heart live inside a young beautiful girl. She said not to let false beauty trick me either, by thinking that it was all I wanted. She said life was easy and complicated at the same time but that God's love was the most basic and easiest thing to accept. I didn't understand or accept what she said. Those were the last words I said to my mother because she died before I was ever able to see her again. I came to the United States and made a more normal life working. I worked for families who were very wealthy compared to the way I grew up. I loved being surrounded by all the pretty things that these families had. I raised their children for them, but their children didn't want me, they wanted their parents. These families did not practice religion and I began to see that these children lacked something. They did not feel loved. This is very sad and ugly. In all this beauty I saw great ugliness. I began to understand my mother's words. Her last words to me taught me a great lesson. I carry these words with me every day and I have made my peace with God.

In this story we can discover multiple meanings to "ugliness," and "beauty." We all relate to these words and are delighted and surprised when their meanings are made new to us again. Images provide us with a parody that moves us into deeper reflection—a spirituality of wisdom.

Jackie (Mexican American), 43 years old

My grandmother was a very special person in my life. I grew up in Texas and we were poor. I was very aware of our status because every day at school I was ostracized by the predominately white children who did not like my clothes, my hair, my skin, my name or my lunches. My little old grandmother would deliver my lunch to me every day. I always had a warm taco with beans and meat or rice and a small thermos of milk. Everyone else had white bread sandwiches with cold cuts. I always felt pained at lunch time because part of me didn't want to see my grandmother and the other part of me felt so guilty for feeling that way. She knew that children made fun of me and of her but she acted as if she was oblivious to it. She always brought certain differences to my attention, never explicitly saying what she really meant but laying a foundation of thought in my head. If a different colored plant grew out of place she would comment on how its difference made things more interesting. She would brush her long hair at night and comment on how some people did not like it when gray hair began to grow into their natural color but she said that she liked it because it meant something different and it gave more strength to her dark hair. She said everything in nature should be appreciated because it was part of God's design. As I got older things did not get any easier. I wondered why my only happy place was in my home when other children got to be happy both in their homes and at school. Finally, things began to change. The Chicano movement began to blossom and I grabbed hold tight to it. I felt like it was my knight in shining armor coming to save me from this cruel society I had grown up in. I became very militant to the point of becoming cruel to those persons who were different from me. I lost my grandmother's words about the importance of differences. I became an angry and sad person. I took a break from the movement because I wanted to think about where I was and

where I was going. By this time my grandmother had been dead five years and I suddenly began to miss her terribly. I began to recall all of my best memories together with her and her knack for always pointing out the beauty of differences in life. I began to think more about her words and they took on more meaning. That was about twenty years ago and today I have finally come full circle. I appreciate myself and others, all thanks to my old, wise grandmother.

If theology is faith reflecting upon life then there is a whole theology here in these stories. In these are "organic" theologians telling us: who this God is, how this God works, what this God does, how dependent they are upon this God and how their life and this God represent the same thing. They are doing theology. But they are not using the scholarly language of the tradition of theology. What emerges is a spirituality that is rooted in reality *as it is* challenging us not to sanitize God but to "see" beyond seeing.

But let me back up a little. To understand Latina women we must appreciate their assumptive world, their psychosocial reality. Furthermore, to understand the effect of any religious experience on a person, or emergent spirituality, we must understand how experience is perceived and valued, and how it motivates behavior. In other words, how it fits into the person's assumptive world and psychosocial reality.

THE PSYCHOSOCIAL DIMENSION

The psychosocial dimension is often considered the primary and exclusive avenue by which individuals understand their world. This dimension is spoken of as containing an assumptive world view which includes intra-psychic life and interpersonal relations. In my book *Our Lady of Guadalupe* I develop what I call a psycho-social religious perspective to understand the Latina woman. This includes assumptions that are formed by perceptions, behaviors, environment, emotional states, values, expectations, and the way a person images not only self but others. This assumptive world view is also influenced by historical events, choices, and social conditioning. The psychosocial dimension, for Latina women, is tightly integrated with the religious dimension. A psychosocial dimension is not a different component from the religious dimension but is inherent in it. The religious dimension or sphere of human experience integrates belief, faith, and behavior in relation to the divine. Given this intrinsic link of the psychosocial and religious, questions previously considered religious must be asked within this broader perspective.

Culture also plays an important role in this

assumptive world. Human beings are social crea-
tures and as such their world view and behavior
are influenced by, perhaps even molded by, the
standards of the groups to which they belong.[15]
Our worldview cannot be divorced from cultural
influences.

The majority of Latinos are Roman Catholic.
Therefore Latinas' psychosocial religious development has been brought about, as well as hindered,
by this legacy of a culturally construed Catholi-
cism. As in most traditional social orders it falls
on Latina women to be the primary carriers of the
religious belief system. The very nature of the
hierarchy of the Roman Catholic Church and of
its traditional teachings has called for women to
be subordinate to men. But this system has not
precluded them from playing an active role in the
practice of popular religiosity. Women are expect-
ed to socialize their children into the cultural
belief systems and instill in them the religious
belief system, including the teachings of the
Roman Catholic Church as they understand them.
For many people in the Hispanic/Latino community, as in general for people who have been marginalized on many levels, the religious world view
is their only world view. They understand everything within a religious context. Latina women
have been marginalized as women, as mestizos,
and as women in a patriarchal society and church.

For Latina women religious and cultural oppression play the major role in the formation of their assumptive world view.

The history, for example, of Mexican American women is a legacy of conquest and resistance. This legacy of conquest and resistance prevalent in many of the Latino cultures shapes the uniqueness of their perceptions, emotional states, images of self, values, gender roles and expectations. A common saying among us is that "the conquista continues."

Despite Latina women's diversity, a number of elements may or may not bind them together. One common element is that, in general, Latina women primarily identify themselves in relation to others, unlike the Western way of thinking of oneself first as an individual and defining oneself through work and roles. Latina women do not separate the fact that they are someone's sister, daughter, mother, friend. Other elements include the desire to (and the belief that we have the right to) maintain our cultural heritage, which we have maintained despite five hundred years of "influence." This heritage includes our language, customs, and ways of perceiving the world and acting in that world.

Throughout history, both in Mexico and in the United States, this right to cultural maintenance has been consistently denied by dominant cultures. "We had learned about the greatness of the

American experience and we hold it in great reverence. What we had not studied were the cruel injustices involved in the process of nation-building [Christianizing, civilizing]: the massacres of the natives, the slave trade, the systematic impoverishment of the Mexican inhabitants of the Southwest."[16] At the base of all these dynamics is the racism, ethnocentrism, and classism deeply ingrained in United States culture.

What makes up the experience of Latina women? Words that come to mind are "conquest" and "resistance," "borderlands," "born and/or raised in the USA." And yet another group of words accompanies the first—words like "integrity," "anger," "pain," "economically and politically marginalized," and "multiple identities." Other women may have multiple identities in terms of their roles, but here I mean something profoundly metaphysical: a woman from a dominant culture does not have to learn another culture's point of view to survive, but Latina women must know the ways of the dominant culture.

Many people, because of the various roles they play, know what it is like to live multiple identities in terms of roles. Here is a description from Gloria Anzaldúa's *Borderlands* [17] of what it is like to cross between cultures that are metaphysically different:

Indigenous like corn, like corn the mestiza is a product of crossbreeding, designed for preservation under a variety of conditions. Like an ear of corn—female seed-bearing organ—the mestiza is tenacious, tightly wrapped in the husks of her culture. Like kernels she clings to the cob; with thick stalks and strong brace roots, she holds tight to the earth—she will survive the crossroads.

This constant crossing becomes the most ordinary thing in Latina women's lives. Although they cross back and forth between these dual identities, they sometimes feel terribly unaccepted—orphaned. Some do not identify with the Anglo-American cultural values. Latina women are the synthesis of these two cultures with varying degrees of acculturation, and with that synthesis comes conflict. They are mestizas biologically, psychologically, and spiritually.

Another powerful insight that comes from the feminist writer Gloria Anzaldúa is that "the future will belong to the Mestizo...because the future depends on the breaking down of paradigms; it depends on the straddling of two or more cultures. By creating a new mythos...the way we see ourselves...the ways we behave...la mestiza creates a new consciousness...the work of mestiza consciousness is to break down the subject-object duality that keeps her a prisoner....."[18]

My intention of sharing these insights is to give the reader a filter through which to receive the next set of stories. You will see that these next stories touch upon factors like: acculturation, popular religiosity, relationship to spirit world, and various forms of oppression (racism, domestic violence, isolation, indifference).

DREAMS, VISIONS AND THE COMMUNION OF SAINTS

The stories that follow contain an oral tradition that opens the portals of time and gives us access to multi-levels of existence. Many native traditions, specifically those with Shamanic elements, are filled with narratives and rituals that concern themselves with the supernatural, the non-ordinary world. As in Native American/medicine stories the boundaries are "not sharp and distinct...so in all stories from the oral traditions, some of the details are from the world we know while other details refer to the supernatural or non-physical universe...many times the stories weave back and forth between the everyday and the supernatural....For those raised in the rationalist world where the linear mind reins supreme, distinctions are mighty. In it there is no possibility— other than the imaginary or psychological....Yet, traditional people insist that conversations with... supernaturals...are actual."[19] In the Latino culture, death is not seen as the final act. For those who believe and for those who love, one can maintain access to, relationship with, connection to, the spirit and the essence of those who have gone before us.

When I was in graduate school I studied under Father Don Gelpi and he said, "The final dualism that needs to be exorcised from a Christian theology of the human is...the dualism of time and eternity."[20] The following stories give witness to struggle, perseverance, faith, and access to various dimensions of existence.

Lydia (Mexican/Puerto Rican), 43 years old

It is not an old story and my mother didn't tell me. But in a sense my mother did tell me. I had it in a dream. My mom said it, you know, but sometimes I questioned whether it was a dream. I've always said that my mother talks to me while I'm sleeping. Well anyway, one night my mother came and got me, she said, "Come, come with me," and she took me to a place that reminded me of Hawaii. The climate was warm, it smelled fragrant, there was the ocean and there was this woman behind us always kind of following us and I kept trying to turn around and see who that was but my mother kept talking to me saying, "Mija, don't worry, you're going to be okay, your dad's going to be okay and everything is going to be okay, and I'm alive." (This is very significant for Lydia because her mother died a very long and painful death due to cancer. She was in excruciating pain and Lydia tells how she remembers her mother praying the rosary and never complaining as tears ran down her face.) She had this radiance about her. She was beautiful. She was whole, healthy, wonderful, the beautiful mother I knew, not the cancerous mother I last saw. She told me that I had to continue loving and I had to continue taking care of things. She told me how proud she was of me and that I had to remember that it was God who gave me all the accomplishments and that now it was my turn to give back to the community. My mother and I continued to walk on the beach and there was this great big rock that we tried to sit on and this lady, this lady that was following us, she was all covered up and she had this radiance about her. And, the closer she got to me the more at peace I felt. Just talking about it I feel this sense of peace and calmness. My mother started rubbing my hair like she did when I was a little girl and all of a sudden this lady touched me and it was like this coziness, I don't know, this beautifulness about it and I looked and I couldn't really see her but I knew she was Nuestra Madre Guadalupe. I mean, I knew it, I just knew it. And I woke up and I turned to my partner and said you know I just talked to my mom and she's okay, and everything's okay. So, the next thing I did was to call my brother and when I called my brother because our birthdays are one week apart he

told me that he had a dream, a dream of when we lived in this old house, how my mother was singing and making Mexican chocolate and I said that's so strange because that's about the same time I had this dream of mom and this lady. I just knew this lady (Guadalupe) was traveling with her and that in her and through her we were all connected even after death.

Lydia's dream is a journey from anxiety to peace. She walks with her mother and all her concerns are brought to a peaceful conclusion. She is disposed to listen to her dream, believing, as she says, "my mother talks to me while I'm sleeping." In the dream there are definite Christological threads of expressions that by themselves may not be significant, but together portray Lydia's mother as both Christ and Virgin. The mother comes for her with the words similar to Jesus' call to his disciples to "come, come with me." The mother's reassuring words ("Mija, don't worry, you're going to be okay, your dad is going to be okay, and everything is going to be okay, and I'm alive") are reminiscent of Jesus' words to Mary Magdalene and the disciples after his resurrection. This remark is especially poignant given the long and painful death the mother had suffered.

Lydia uses the word radiance to describe both her mother and the Virgin of Guadalupe. She sees in her mother the same qualities she sees in the

Virgin. The mother gave her a message to "continue loving" and "taking care of things," to remember that "all accomplishments come from God,"
and that it is time for her to give something back to
the community. This is reminiscent of Jesus giving
his last instructions to the apostles before his ascen-
sion. Walking together along the beach reempha-
sizes the intimacy and what we call in Spanish
"acompañamiento," accompaniment of the mother with her daughter. In retelling the dream Lydia
says that she re-experiences the "sense of peace and
calm." There is a sensuous aspect to the dream with
smells, beautiful sights, touch, warmth, along with
the vague presence of a mysterious other that later
is known to be Our Lady of Guadalupe. And then
in a final epiclesis the narration ends with Lydia
confident and unafraid because Guadalupe "was
traveling with her, in her and through her" in a
bond that connects "even after death." This narration of a dream exemplifies the unconscious incor-
poration of Christological themes into the death
and "new life" of a deceased mother which in turn
give hope and meaning to a surviving daughter.
Lydia in her dream and her interpretation has fash-
ioned a spirituality that brings together, in a mean-
ingful way, elements important to her as a woman,
as an Hispanic, and as a Christian. Would that we
could spend more time with her and many others

41

like her to bring to consciousness and greater clarity that spirituality that is uniquely hers.

Raquel (Mexican American), 44 years old

This is a story about my mother and my grandmother because when I was born it was during World War II and we lived with our grandparent. I must have been about six years old and I remember having this dream and in the dream, it was just so vivid, a woman came to me, a woman I'd never seen. She came to me and she told me to tell, I think it was to tell my mother, that everything was okay and that people should stop crying and that my mother should tell someone else to stop crying. They weren't supposed to cry anymore. And I remember what she looked like and the next day I described her to my mother and my grandmother who were in the kitchen. And as I was telling them about this woman and about the dream, my grandmother asked me to describe her and what she looked like. I described her and I don't remember all the exact words but what I remember my grandmother and my mother looking at each other and kind of nodding like that nod that they kind of knew and understood. It turned out I was describing an aunt who had died, who I didn't know. Anyway they knew who she was and they knew that the message needed to be passed on.

That was for her children and the message was because someone was grieving so much and she wanted them to know that they could stop grieving, that it was all right, they didn't have to cry so much. And the significant thing about the story is that she's dead. And why should a dead person be talking to me, I asked. And both my mother and my grandmother said well that's normal and that's the way life is. Sometimes people come to you in your dreams or they come to you in visions and it is their way of communicating with other people. It is perfectly all right and nothing to be afraid of. *Es parte de la vida.* It is part of life. So I grew up thinking that there was nothing wrong with this cross-world communication.

Raquel's narration is also a dream where a woman comes to her with a calming message that everything is okay and that people should stop crying. This type of dream is very common in the Hispanic community, especially after the death of someone in the family. In the narration the place for interpreting the dream is in the kitchen. Raquel is there with her mother and grandmother. It is in the kitchen that the meaning of the dream is revealed and that a lesson of life is learned, which is that sometimes people come to you in dreams and visions, and "that's the way life is." Older women instruct the younger women. And messages received in a dream must be passed on to those who know and understand. Key to this narration is the impact that this event had in Raquel's life as a result of not only the dream but also the interpretation of the older women. She concludes with, "So I grew up thinking that there was nothing wrong with this cross-world communication." Such a statement is a building block to a particular world view and set of assumptions. It is this kind of assumption that makes it possible for one to see spiritual significance in life events.

Sonja (Mexican American), 79 years old

I was working at the time in a small town in Arizona. I was twenty-one years old at the time and I remember I had to walk about seven miles to get home and I remember arriving home and asking my dad, "Where's mom?" And he said, "Well, she went to church." It was already dark and I said, "How did she go to church?" And so I went over and got her. I went to the church and I picked her up and I said, "How could you walk in the dark? You have to go on railroad tracks and the church is up on a large hill." It was Our Lady of Guadalupe church. And she said, "I walked but it wasn't dark." She said, "No, no it wasn't dark." She said, "All the way to the church there was a light right in front of me." I said, "For heaven's sake, isn't that something!" But she said she had to go to the rosary that evening and you know that is always the one thing that stuck in my mind about that. She said there was a light just in front of her those five miles to that church. I don't know. Was it la Virgin? Was it the light of faith? I don't know, but there were no lights back then.

Sonja's story reveals a passive father, a determined mother and a concerned daughter. The mother's experience of a light guiding her path results in the daughter's amazement. The inference in the story is that the mother's faith and commitment to the rosary brought with it a safe journey to the church. Sonja's questions at the end of her story reveal that after many years she is still searching for an explanation. It is that searching that leads one to explore a religious response.

Sylvia (Mexican, first generation), 53 years old

The stories that I remember my mother telling me are stories just from her growing up. My grandparents were illegal aliens from Mexico and they sneaked across the border and took refuge in a mission in Arizona. My grandmother was twelve years old, my grandfather fifteen years old when they got married. People used to say that my mother looked like Merle Oberon. She would tell a lot of stories about her growing up. Maybe she just needed to process them for herself. Maybe she just needed to get it out. But I think my mom had a lot of suffering in her life and she needed to talk about it. I mean you are right in the middle of it, you're trying to cope and you're trying to deal with all these different things just trying to survive. I remember things that she would tell me. She would tell me, "You need to learn how to type." And she taught all of us how to type really well at five, six or seven years old. We had this big old portable thing and I remember making designs with the typewriter and lining up the words and the letters. But I remember her very distinctly telling us, my brother and my sister alike, "You've got to learn how to type—you've just got to learn how to type because you will always be able to get a job wherever you go and you will always be very independent and you won't have to depend on anybody for your financial security." Maybe the reason she told us so much about the difficulties that she had was that she didn't want us to work in a restaurant, or the cannery, or in the fields. My mom told me this story and made me learn how to type because she didn't want me to have the same hard life that she had.

Sylvia's story illustrates a common memory of Latina women: their mothers "suffering," enduring many "difficulties," and living a "hard life." It is from this struggle that mothers teach their children to survive, to become independent, and to seek financial security. This type of memory is by no means unique to Latina women but it brings Latinas into solidarity with many others whose commitment to improving their lot is a result of the wisdom and the "consejos" of parents who have lived a hard life.

Tére (Chicana, Arizona), 39 years old

Well recently I went to my grandmother's 89th birthday and she's really strong. One of the things that I remember hearing at the birthday celebration is the following:

Now this grandmother is my dad's mother and she got married at a very young age. And she had about fourteen or fifteen children. My aunt told us that the one thing my grandma never told the grandchildren is that instead of being raised pulling everything, we could have been raised with a little bit of money because her boyfriend, when she was a teenager, was the owner of J.C. Penney. And so my cousin said, "Grandma, you mean all this time I could have been shopping?" Well, we said, how did that come to be? She said, "Oh, I'd always go downtown and he'd always say he wanted to date me or wanted to marry me, but I would never do it because he wasn't a Mexican." And so that was something new I had learned about my grandma. The other thing I remember is that she remembers everything. There are lots and lots of people we saw at the family gathering; we had hundreds of folks there, and she remembered everyone by name. But the one thing that had always struck me about her is that even though she had had a very traumatic time just this year—she lost one of her sons—she would always tell us that things would happen *si dios quiere* (if God wants). So it always struck me that no matter what we do or want to do, it is always another being that is going to determine what actually happens or that tells us we should be concerned about what happens. And so, the thing that I remember about my grandmother was her face and the fact that she was a strong woman.

This story contains several themes that are common in many recollections about Latina mothers and grandmothers. One is that the grandmother is described as "really strong," referring to her strength of character. This story speaks to this issue by referring to the grandmother's face, and stating that "she was a strong woman." This is usually the result, as in this case, of a difficult life. Another theme that is important and common to many Latinos is the notion of "God's will": *Si dios quiere*. In some of the literature dealing with the psychology of Latinos, this expression is often referred to as reflective of an attitude of resignation or fatalism. This conclusion is supported by

the statement we find in the story that "no matter what we do or want to do it is always another being that is going to determine what actually happens...." This attitude goes against the American philosophy of rugged individualism and limitless possibilities. While one attitude may be overly deterministic, the other smacks of naive narcissism.

Rosemary (Mexican American), 31 years old

Well, for me the one thing that I learned from my mom is that it doesn't matter where you live. It's how you live. My mom was born in Mexico. When she was very young she and her sister basically helped raise her other two brothers. Lots of the stories she tells me are stories of when they came to the United States and when they did migrant work. You know they used to live in barns. You know how they have the stalls for the animals in the barn? Every family had a place in there; that's where they put them. I said to my mom, "How did you fit?" You know there was my mom, my aunt, my grandfather, her two brothers—how could that many people fit into a stall? She said that the growers would find a stall based on your family and size of your family and that was where you lived when you came to work in the fields. "Well," I said, "how did you guys eat and all that?" And she said that in the middle of the barn they would do a fire pit and everyone would go and cook their meals. "Well, how did you wash your clothes?" I'd ask. She said there were many times that they had to go out to the river and wash their clothes. That has always struck me because now I understand that it didn't matter whether we lived in a one-bedroom or whether we lived in Washington. To her it was more important *how* you lived.

This story highlights the common themes of the struggles and hard times of migrant families moving from Mexico to the United States. Again the mother is seen as strong and determined to survive. The daughter living in very difficult circumstances is aided by the mother's words of focusing on "how" one lives, not where.

Rachel (second-generation Mexican American), 41 years old

I was in the kitchen and we had had some people over for dinner. It was around ten o'clock at night and I had just put my children to sleep when all of a sudden a dog started barking. And, oh God, she was driving me crazy and she ran upstairs and I said, "Just a second, let me go see what's going on." I didn't want her waking up the baby, so I ran up the first flight of stairs and the dog was barking by my daughter's room.

Just as I got to the first landing I looked up and you know I felt something. I felt something and I looked up and I saw a shadow go across the hall—down the hall like from her room to my son's room, and it was like I felt there was a message here. There is something here I need to understand. I tried not to be afraid. I went up to my daughter's room; she was crying but she was sound asleep. She was crying in her sleep. So I checked her to see if she was okay and she was fine. As soon as I patted her, touched her, she stopped crying. I said there's something here that's not good. Then I went in and checked on my boys and the boys were fine.

I came downstairs and I told my husband and the guests that were at the house what was going on and the dog finally stopped barking, and I finally calmed down. But it was strange, and I could see the hair on the back of the dog's neck kind of stand up. Anyway, I was scheduled to leave the next day to go to a meeting north of Missoula and I said you know I really think there's a message in anything that just happens; I just know there is. I don't think it's an evil spirit, but I think there's definitely a message. My husband had already gone through this stuff with me before, and he said, "It will come to you." I had trouble sleeping that night. But all of a sudden it just came to me. Stay home. You're not to go on the road; you're not to go on this trip. Death will happen if you go on this trip. So when I woke up the next morning I just decided I'm not going on a trip. This is a sign and I'm not going. I went and as I started to get up and get ready it turned out to be snowing. It was a freak snow storm. I don't know how many inches of snow but there had been all kinds of accidents on the roads, on the back roads I was supposed to be traveling on. I was supposed to be driving myself in this crazy Volkswagen van with slick tires. So of course I called my mother. I don't know if my mother remembers this. But I told her the whole thing and she told me to go down to the church and get some holy water and to remember to say my prayers and bring the prayers and the water to each corner of the room. You know, everywhere where I had seen the spirit. So that's what I did. As my children grew older I shared this story with them because it is important that they know not to be frightened because sometimes we get messages from people who have gone before and who love us. I wasn't using the holy water as a way of exorcising the spirit. I was using it as a way of thanking the spirit. Sometimes a spirit gets agitated and needs to rest and holy water gives it a chance to rest. I feel like I might have been dead by now if I

hadn't paid attention. So I guess it's really important, and I'm grateful for coming from a culture that recognizes this and kind of sees it as a blessing.

Rachel's story of the barking dog begins with a sense that there was something "not good" in the house and with a premonition that "there was a message." As in other stories there is a predisposition to such messages because of the belief that "sometimes we get messages from people who have gone before and who love us." Isabel receives and heeds the message as a warning against a planned trip. In the end she interprets the experience as a blessing. After consultation with her mother she is told to sprinkle holy water and say prayers where she had seen the spirit. This story is passed on to her children, presumably with a warning to pay attention to the spirit world. Isabel's story shows the predisposition to the religious world view that exists in the Hispanic community. Barring any other explanations, this predisposition allows the person to make sense of the world and continue to function. While the emergence of rationalism and scientific investigation has been operative since the middle of the eighteenth century, most people interpret their world from a religious perspective. Most Hispanics are no different.

Isabel (third generation Mexican-American), 33 years old

This is a story that my mother told me when I was nine years old. I walked into the kitchen and my mom just seems to have this look of hope in her face. She was going through a really tough time in the family. Mom had a lot of struggles and my dad was, well you know, he was struggling with alcohol, and mom just had to be extra tough. You know there were eleven of us in the family. In any case she told me that she had this dream. She was outside hanging clothes and all of a sudden it was like the sky had just opened up and the clouds had just kind of separated and there was this great light. She could see the Lord and with him were his apostles and it was the most beautiful sight she had ever seen. I've interpreted the story as a sign that there is a light at the end of a tunnel because my mom was, well, she was just down and somehow this dream just reassured her that these tough times were going to pass. I could just see it in her face that she was ready to start a brand new day. So when I have my struggles with, you know, career or marriage, or something like that, I just think of that story and I remember that the sun will shine tomorrow; that tomorrow will be another day.

Isabel's story brings with it the familiar themes of the mother in the kitchen, a mother who has lots of struggles but still has hope. The father also has struggles, but his are related to alcohol abuse which means that mom "had to be extra tough." Men in many of these stories are portrayed as weak, passive, or non-existent. Robbed of their identity and dignity in this western individualistic culture, they cannot function as responsible men. It is no wonder that mother's dream is of idealized men in the person of Jesus and of his apostles. They are a beautiful sight that take Isabel's mother away from the mundane chore of hanging clothes. The result is a feeling of "reassurance," not only for the mother who had the dream, but also for the daughter who remembers her mother's dream. The story/dream has a transformative impact upon the daughter and helps her be optimistic in times of her own struggles. Women sharing their dreams and stories with one another can have an uplifting and affirming effect on one another. They create the bonds of friendship necessary in a religious community. I dare say that when men do the same thing, a similar result will happen.

Teresa (Puerto Rican), 32 years old

This is a story that my grandmother told us. She told us this in order to teach us about sharing and to tell us that there's always enough food for everyone. I was about sixteen years old when she told us. She said there was once a person who never served anyone in the house a meal if there was someone visiting. This woman one day was in her house cooking when she had some guests but she didn't offer her guests anything. She didn't serve them anything. She didn't offer them anything. So she waited until they left and then when she decided to serve the food to people in her house, she lifted the lid on the pot of beans and what she found in there was a bunch of black worms! My grandmother also told me how one day my grandmother and grandfather had unexpected guests. My grandmother was concerned that there wasn't enough food to serve everyone. But my grandfather asked her to serve the food and to serve the guests first. My grandmother was very preoccupied and nervous but she served them anyway and what she discovered was that there was enough food for everyone. She doesn't understand how it was that she kept taking rice out of the pot but there was still more rice. Since that time my grandmother has taught us to bless the food and to make the sign of the cross over the pot before serving from it. This assures us that the food will be sufficient for all those who arrive.

Josie (Puerto Rican), 35 years old

This story my grandmother, who has already died, told me when I was in Puerto Rico. I was about six or seven years old and she told me the story because I didn't want to share my candies with my cousin. My grandmother was about seventy years old when she told me this story. She had told this story to my mother as well:

There was a woman who didn't share anything with anybody and if some visitor came to the house she would cover the pot and wait until they left before she would serve her family. But one day a visitor arrived and stayed at the house for a very long time. It was very late and it was night-time when the visitor finally left. And so, the family went to bed without eating. One of the members of the family got up to eat. She lit a candle and went to the kitchen to get something out of the pot but when she opened the lid she found a snake inside. The woman from that day forward never covered the food from anyone again.

These two stories highlight hospitality as a key value for a Christian way of life. Unlike the other stories, in the first story it is the grandfather that insists upon adherence to the value whereas the grandmother is worried that there might not be enough food. It is the confidence of the grandfather that helps the grandmother discover the abundance of food they had to share. Thereafter, the grandmother blesses the food before serving it and teaches others to do the same. In this story the blessing of food is not an act of thanksgiving but a prayer that there will be enough for all that are hungry. Serving food becomes an act of faith. It is constitutive of the spirituality of these women that they celebrate the presence of their God in the day-to-day tasks of cooking, washing, and caring for children. Their stories are not of things that happen inside a church building or a convent, but in the mundane activities of their day and the dreams of their nights. The stories they share are a theology of incarnation wherein the divine becomes intimately connected with daily human activities and expressed in the language of common understanding. While this is not to limit women's spirituality to the context of household tasks, it is the context of the vast majority of women and thus understandable that women seek meaning and hope within that situation. Again it is our task as theologians to bring the subtleties of that context and that search for the divine to consciousness and thus to affirmation and critical dialogue.

Elba (Puerto Rican), 43 years old

I remember my mother telling me that one must conform to what God has given us. When I was little she used to say, "She who laughs last, laughs more." She also said that she'd discovered that's not always true. She would tell me stories about how when her parents were going through town to buy food they would come back to divide it among the family, which was twelve children. Many times when they divided up the pieces, the last person to get a piece either got a very small piece or sometimes no piece at all. My mother used to always tell us that when we had meat not to eat our meat last, because if guests arrived then we would have to give our meat to the guests. Today I have two daughters and I try to teach them not only that they need to share, but to conform themselves to what God has given them.

Elba's story is a paradoxical call to conformity to "what God has given..." and to practical advice in anticipation of having a guest over for dinner, i.e., eat your meat first so as to not have to share if guests arrive. This clever twist on the rule of hospitality assumes first that there is such a rule and then plays on it to get children to eat their food. It reflects the importance of the custom of hospitality in our culture. This folk adage is not unlike the rule of St. Benedict that if a guest arrives during the solemn recitation of the office, one or more of the brothers is to stop and attend to the guest as another Christ.

Magdalena (Puerto Rican), 36 years old

A story I remember vividly was told to me by my Godmother. The day of my first Holy Communion, she came to my house before the ceremony to help me get ready. She said, "Make sure your thoughts are all pure ones today and that you confess all your sins to the priest. If you don't, the host you swallow won't have anyplace to go in your heart. It will keep searching for a 'clean' spot to settle in your heart." When she told me this I could really "see" the host swimming around inside me looking for a spot that was clean and free of sin.

Magdelena's story of the host swimming around looking for a "clean spot to settle in your heart" is typical of imaginative stories children were told to keep them in line. While this one is relatively harmless, there are others told of our sins putting another nail in the hands of Jesus, or of our souls becoming black and ugly with each sin we commit. The intention was to help children take seriously their participation in the supper of the Lord. Unfortunately many times these images did more to instill guilt, shame, and a sense of unworthiness that only grew with time and normal human development. Not all learned stories are life-giving. Not all memories lead to growth. Again, sharing the stories with others objectifies them and allows for critical reflection.

Vicki (Mexican-American), 41 years old

My mother passed away about nine years ago when she was a junior in college. We're talking about a fifty-seven year old woman who decided to go back to school in her fifties. I mean, here's somebody who is going after college and a degree and it was just for the purpose of self-improvement, you know. If I had to point to any one person in my life who I can say the reason I've accomplished certain things is because of them, that "them" would be my mom. I was her first born and she invested a lot in me and always wanted me to have the highest of aspirations. Sometimes I made her proud and sometimes I think I probably disappointed her. But I remember being real small driving the car and she'd say, "Okay, you're going to go to college, right?" And I'd say, "yeah," not really knowing what college was. Then she'd say, "You have three choices: what do you want to be—a doctor, lawyer, or an engineer?" Well, none of them really sounded interesting and I had no idea what I wanted to be. I was probably only in first or second grade, but she would tell me about all these women engineers and women doctors and that I could do it if I wanted to. I could do any-

thing if I wanted to. My mother wanted that for me. She was always a working woman and she was a smart woman, but because of her lack of education there were certain limits as to how far she could go. She didn't want that for me.

Vicki's memory of her mother is a mixture of admiration, ambition and guilt at not living up to her expectations. Her comment, "I think I probably disappointed her" is understandable, given the high expectations placed upon her. Her admission that "I had no idea what I wanted to do" reveals a possible fear of failure and a lack of affirmation that whatever she would choose would be okay. These parental attitudes are often transferred to God, and one can easily live life in a constant state of shame at not meeting up to the unrealisitic expectations or one's perception of God.

Becky (Ecuadoran), 35 years old

My mom didn't so much tell me stories, per se, but we had a lot of conversations about her growing up. She was orphaned at age twelve; she lost both her mother and father and she had a very difficult life. She was terribly naive and very unsophisticated and uneducated. My mother went to live with her aunts but her aunts made her do the cooking and cleaning and things like that. Finally, she decided she just couldn't take

this anymore. She wanted something different so she went to the local priest and the priest managed to get some money together and put her on a bus to the capital, where she tried looking for her extended family. But nobody could take her in. So finally she came to the United States and became a nanny to a family, and she worked for months and worked two jobs and just really had a hard time making it on her own. So she would tell me these stories about her being abandoned as a child by her extended family, and how scary it was for her. At some point though she wrote a letter to her family in South America just to let them know that she was okay. Despite the fact that she felt abandoned by them she never thought to get herself educated. She never did anything to really help herself. She always sort of took on an attitude of humility, and it took her a long time, but eventually she forgave her family. What drove her to forgive them was that they started to write letters to each other. More importantly, it was because of my birth. When I started growing up and asking who my family was, and where my grandparents or parents were, she realized that she had to reconnect me to my family and my culture. So in a way I guess I was responsible for bringing her back to her family, because she realized how much we needed them, even though she kind of rejected them because she'd felt so hurt. She was willing to forgive for the sake of her children. These stories that my mother told me, and her reconciliation with her family, had an impact on me. The one thing that it taught me was the importance of family. Another lesson I got out of the story she told me was that you never tell a child anything that you do not intend on seeing all the way through. When you tell a child you're going to do something, you have to keep your word because with children everything you say is gospel. They believe everything you say; you have to be sensitive to that. Children are inno- cent and should be protected and feel loved. So these are the kinds of things that she would tell me about her life and what she'd learned. Having been raised in the United States, I know that I would never want to be in a position where I couldn't defend myself or be independent. I also know that I don't want to be without my family.

Becky's story of her orphaned mother is yet another tale of hardship and abandonment expe- rienced by a woman who is abused and forsaken, even by her extended family. It is curious that Becky sees her also as a person who "never did anything to really help herself." She does acknowl- edge that her mother forgave her family for what they had done to her. Still Becky sees even this act of reconciliation as resulting from her influence.

Nonetheless, the mother puts aside her hurt to seek reconciliation and in this action teaches her daughter the "importance of family." She also learns that "children are innocent and should be protected and feel loved." Becky concludes by affirming the importance of defending oneself, one's independence, and family life. These are values that have emerged from other stories and are repeated here. This repetition of similar values leads to the conclusion that these are not just the values of individuals but also those of a whole culture. The negative experiences of these women only reinforce the desire to have their children live out these values. They are values that are passed on from one generation of women to another and, as stated previously, seem to form a constitutive part of their spirituality.

Yolanda (second-generation Mexican-American), 36 years old

Whenever I felt discouraged or down about something, my mom would tell me a story that she would take out of her own life. She used to say how much she loved education and relished going to school, partly because it was the one place she got away from many of the problems of her family, like alcoholism. She loved school and she loved to excel. In fourth grade she was in a class where she was at the top level. But when she

moved into fifth grade she was the only Mexican-American in the class and the teacher decided that Mexican-Americans weren't smart enough to be in the top level class, and so she was demoted two levels. In that class were all Mexican students and he said that that's where she belonged. She studied very diligently and hard; she made good grades and even though she would be doing well the teacher would still grade her down and she suffered very much during that year. Then when she passed on to sixth grade, the teacher in the sixth grade wanted to pass her on to the upper level because, the teacher said, it was clear she didn't belong there. She was functioning well academically and in the course of two or three months she was once again in the top level class. So the stories my mom told me were clear examples of racism and they helped me not to be discouraged. She told me how important it was to believe in yourself and in the gifts that you bring. She was determined to work very hard and not let anyone pull her down. You know, a lot of students that my mom went to school with had opportunities to take piano, to take horseback riding lessons, or whatever. But my mom was poor and she couldn't do those things. But the one thing that my mother could do was go to the library, because it was free. She spent a lot of time in the library. That was the one activity she could participate in. My mom is the only one out of six children in her family that ultimately went to college. I am grateful for her stories that nurtured me and helped me determine to reach for the stars.

Yolanda tells us a story told her by her mother. Like the others we have heard, it is one of dashed hopes and struggles, both in the family and in school. The lesson learned is to believe in one's self and in one's gifts. A story of determination and suffering is one of nurturance and inspiration.

Gaby (Mexican/El Salvadoran), 32 years old

My mom always said you should be proud of who you are. I think the reason she said this is because she wanted to make sure that whatever you did, whatever job you had, you should not be ashamed of it, as long as you know it's an honest job. There are a lot of people like you who ask, "What do you do?" and you say, "Well, I clean houses," and they say, "Oh, you like them"—you know what I mean. I think what my mom taught me was that it doesn't matter if it's a small job, big job, or not an important job, because I really believe that every job is important because one has to do it, and so sometimes the littlest job you do is the most important because without the little job you're doing, other things wouldn't

work. My mom always said what you do reflects on who you are, whether people think of it as that or not.

Gaby's recollection of her mother's advice reinforces the values of pride in one's self, honest work, and work well done. She warns against being ashamed of one's work and concludes with her mom's admonition "that whatever you do reflects on who you are...." It is clear that Gaby has remembered her mother's teachings and is able to repeat them in a succinct manner. This ability bespeaks of a relationship of careful dialogue and instruction.

Rebecca A. Salgado

I was born here in San Diego on May 15, 1974, but I was raised in a small town in Imperial County called Calexico. Calexico lies on the border between the United States and Mexico; our neighbor city is the capitol of Baja California, Mexicali. I was baptized into the Roman Catholic faith on June 14, 1974 in the Parish of Our Lady of Guadalupe. I have always been surrounded by Guadalupe, and Guadalupe has and is still a very influential part of my life. As well as being baptized in the Parish of Our Lady of Guadalupe, I also received the sacraments of confession, first holy communion and confirmation there. I also

went to the parish parochial school, which was called Our Lady of Guadalupe Academy, from kindergarten to eighth grade. I have been so immersed in Guadalupe for so long. But the Guadalupe that has had the greatest effect on me has been my Nana Lupe.

My Nana was born in Gaston, Arizona. She came to Calexico, California when she was in second grade. She was raised by a very strong woman herself, which just proves that strong women run in my family. My Nana has been the greatest influence in my life. She is the one who introduced me to the Virgen de Guadalupe. If it wasn't for her, I believe that I wouldn't have had the guidance that I had. I credit my Nana for the faith that I have now.

I was raised by my grandparents while my mom was finishing law school. My Nana was the constant that was always there. I believe that there is a bond between us that no one can take away. The bond of faith is especially strong, I believe. All of the twenty-four grandchildren that my Nana has she has tried to involve in the faith. But out of those twenty-four I am the oldest, and the only one who seems to have my Nana's faith: faith in God, faith in miracles, faith in forgiveness, and faith in humanity.

Growing up I can remember the medallions that each of us had—a relatively big gold medallion that had the Virgen de Guadalupe on one side and an image of the Virgin Mary on the other side. We always held December 12 close to our hearts. That was my Nana's feast day. I remember one December 12 when I was in the second grade and my school was having the feast day celebration. I was honored to get to read at Mass. I can still remember my Nana's face as she watched her eight year old granddaughter walk up to the altar and read. Her face beamed with pride. That is one of the best memories I have.

My Nana's faith is unbelievably strong. She has been through so much: the death of a child, the restructuring of her life after my Tata was forced out of his job, raising ten children as well as at least five grandchildren. Recently, though, her faith has been tested many ways, one by the birth of twins. My aunt had twin girls who were born very sickly and she was told they wouldn't live past forty-eight hours. My Nana prayed and all that she asked was that the Lord's will be done— whether that meant taking the children or letting them live. Well, faith is stronger than medicine. Through the help of all the doctors and the faith that my Nana has, the twins will be three this June. More recently, though, her faith was tested by the heart attack that my Tata had. My grandparents have been married for over forty years. Losing my Tata would have been a tremendous blow for all of us. But my Nana's faith is so strong that even though her children were bickering among themselves, and her husband was lying in a hospital bed awaiting the results of what will be, she prayed. My aunts and uncles still bicker. I don't think that will ever stop, but my Tata is still with us and will be for a while. Every night my grandparents pray a rosary and they try to include as many people as possible. I relish those nights with my grandparents. Those are sacred moments that can never be taken away from me.

My Nana has even interceded for me with my trials. I know there are nights when I am constantly in her prayers. I am her only grandchild at a university. But I know that Mary is watching over me and interceding for me. I can feel it.

I can remember each room in my Nana's home having a crucifix. And in my room, even to this day, there is a painting of Our Lady of Guadalupe. My Nana is a Guadalupana. She has an enormous devotion to her, as have most of her children, and one special grandchild (that's me).

Rebecca's long story brings up the familiar theme of Our Lady of Guadalupe, but as in the other stories, she too identifies Guadalupe not only with the Virgin Mary but also with someone in her family who has inspired her. In this case, her grandmother. Again "strong woman" is used to describe not only the grandmother but also other women in this family. Related to this strength is the "guidance" and the passing on of faith to the granddaughter. As in some of the other stories, this faith is manifested as belief in the Virgin of Guadalupe. It is also expressed as faith in God, miracles, forgiveness, and in humanity. These are all themes that have surfaced again and again in the stories of these women. Another recurring theme is that of "the Lord's will be done." Like the remarkable Job of the Hebrew scriptures, Rebecca's grandmother prays for the health of two grandchildren, ever mindful of her relationship to God. Time spent with grandparents is called a "sacred moment." The church has its sacred Sundays and holy hours, but these women also claim as sacred the time spent with one another.

(Mexican-American), 46 years old

My family were sharecroppers. Worked for a white family but they (my parents) had some of their own land, so although they suffered some prejudice, they were more or less isolated.

My dad was a practicing Catholic. Mom, she was baptized. They got married and she started going to church. They're real particular about going to Mass and doing things for the church. When we were little, there were all these parades. I remember the big statue of Our Lady of Guadalupe and the four bearers holding it up, the kids and adults, and singing all the songs in Spanish. The tunes I recognize, but the words, I have to see them. Candles. Always a picture of Our Lady of Guadalupe in the house. We had a picture in the bedroom, statues all over the place.

I never knew my grandmothers.

They (my parents) lived across from an older couple that I knew. They only knew Spanish. She probably knew herbs, and also massage. So whenever we had sore ankles or something my mother would take us to her and she'd rub us and massage us. She was a little, short, motherly, chubby lady that I really loved. She didn't speak English. She taught me to crochet—well, with the needle and a string.

Being part of a family was real big in our family. Family supports family. When we were little, mom had a little preschool, before preschools were in, and she'd have us out in our little playhouse that my dad had made. She'd teach us our colors and numbers. I hated it. I wanted to play.

When I was in high school my mom was in the hospital; my dad was just lost. I think that happens a lot. Especially now that we talk about women's lib and all that. Women do so much in the home but they never get credit for it. It seemed like the man was doing everything, but the woman was behind it. When my mom was sick and in the hospital, my dad, he didn't know, but she paid the bills. I remember that now. He was a carpenter. He had a rack for all the bills so that he could see them all—go down the line and see which ones had to be paid. He didn't know when they were due and all that stuff. He didn't know until then what had to be paid. We didn't have a checking account or anything like that, and I remember my mom always getting money orders. When she got sick he was doing a little bit of that, and then when she got well she was doing it again.

We didn't realize it then, but looking back I see how much we took her for granted, because we were lost (when she was sick).

The story of this sharecropper family seems representative of many. A life lived working the land, suffering some prejudice and participating in the popular religiosity of the Mexican people. It is simple and fairly straightforward: Mass, things for the church, religious processions, statues, music, candles, pictures, and of course Our Lady of Guadalupe. In all this the author learns the importance of family life. She also presents her mother as the center of the family and when the mother is sick both dad and children feel "lost." Family life, religious life and the role of the mother seem intricately interwoven to form the fabric of family life. It is clear that the mother's presence is seen by a number of the women to be the key thread that holds the family together. In some cases more emphasis is placed on the grandmother's presence. It seems reasonable to assume that while the priest is central to the liturgical life of the institutional church it is the mother who is most often the center of the domestic church. Unlike the priest, the mother is also often the center of economic and social life of the family as well.

Suzanna (first generation Mexican-American), 26 years old

Your family is always the most important thing. I think my mom thinks that in the United States people don't always teach that or think that. Now that I am a mom this strikes me more. When I was younger I thought, "You don't want me to go out." Now I know that she wanted to spend time with me. She wanted me to do things with my family, and appreciate my family. It makes me be the mom I am for my son and be the best mom I can.

I feel my mom sacrificed a lot for me. She was on her own for six or seven years. She is not too proud but she is very independent, and I know that my dad didn't really pay child support or anything. I feel that I can be very independent and I follow her in that way.

As far as religion goes, mother and me personally have had times that were hard: my parents' divorce, her remarriage, my sister born after me being an only child for a long time. Mom always said that God's never going to give you anything you can't handle. You'll be okay.

Having a baby at first is so hard and so scary. When I was pregnant, I wasn't ready to be pregnant and I was so scared. I saw it as being punished for doing something I wasn't supposed to be doing, and not as a gift. At first mom was angry. Then she saw it as a gift and that God wants me to have this baby now. She told me that God will always take care of me and be there for me and it'll always work out. Might be scary, but it'll be okay.

It was just me and her for a long time. We had no family in Washington. I used to think, what if something happens to my mom? What will happen to me? My mom had to work and I'd have to be by myself. Mom would tell me, "God will protect you and take care of you. You are never alone. God is always with you," and that is always with me. It is not a conscious thought, or something that I have to think about; it's just there. She planted it in me.

I know that no matter what happens, she'll (mom) always be there for me, and now I'm trying to instill that in my son.

Suzanna affirms the importance of the family in her first sentence. She strives to be like her mother, strong and independent. From her she learns some basic beliefs about God not giving you something you cannot handle, including a baby. Her statement that you are never alone refers both to God and to her mother. In the face of the absent father her confidence lies with her mother and with her God. Suzanna sees this as a message learned from her mom and one she hopes to pass on to her son. The abiding presence of God and her mother is a strong theme in this story and in others. It does not seem that these women are angry at God because of the passivity or abandonment of their fathers. Rather they seem to quite easily find in God those attributes that they see in their mothers. Perhaps because of their mothers' strength, wisdom, presence, and love, God's parental image remains intact and even is enhanced and expanded.

In closing it is clear to me that women's experience can be and is revelatory of the divine.[21] The strongest insight that these stories bring to the surface for me is that of a kind of organic world view that these women have. They seem to be capable of moving with great ease in different worlds, in different ways of being. They are not primarily analytical. They just live. The world is here, it's real and it serves them. They are the creators and subjects of this world. It's a reciprocal dynamic. The world creates them, and they support, encourage and create the world. What may strike the reader about these stories is how broad the community is. Giving back to the community tends to encompass a much broader scope of people than our notion of community as neighborhood, let's say, or even parish. The community that they seem to embrace includes both the living and the dead, the community of saints as well as the extended family. Many of these stories emphasize strength; whether they (the authors) have to be strong, or their moms were strong or their grandmothers were strong. And one might ask what makes these women so strong? What is it that makes them feel that being strong is absolutely what they are called to be? Is it because their mothers were strong? Their grandmothers? Are women strong partly because the men in their lives are not?

The women are strong in a variety of different ways. Although these women have great strength and independence, this does not preclude demonstrated dependence. This is a dependence on family and community, on being loved and being supported. There is this creative tension between dependence and independence. In the dominant society we tend to be educated away from being dependent. We're scared of dependency. In the

Latino world dependence is taken for granted. It is part of their world and part of their organic view. Maybe there's something we can learn here: that it is possible to be dependent and independent at the same time, and to be so in a healthy way. It reminds me of a spirituality of creaturehood where we learn that as God's creation we are both dependent and independent.

Another theme that emerges is how women live vicariously through their children. It seems that all the things that they wanted for themselves and they couldn't get they want for their children. They will do anything to make that happen. In many ways the women's lives have been controlled by outside forces that have forced them into hardship, into a lack of control over their life. They seem determined not to allow this to happen to their children. They are going to control the destiny of their children. They are going to work hard and sacrifice in order to make circumstances better for them. A family of sharecroppers, first-generation immigrants, native born Latinos will emerge out of a racist dominant culture hopefully with a new consciousness—that chooses the best from the two cultures they straddle. The destiny of their children is tied up with the giving up of their lives because this is one of the main purposes in life. They are the daily martyrs. They give up their lives for their children. I know this can be interpreted as morbid, as masochistic, in our modern society. But aren't they closer to living the way we all aspire to do—as disciples of Jesus, who lived entirely for others?

By allowing themselves to feel the impact of their situation of suffering and oppression, whether it is theirs personally, or that of their people, they enter into a moment where they discover God present among them in their very suffering. Not only do they discover God among the outcasts, among the marginalized, and the rejected, but they find a God that asks them to work and do all in their power to relieve the situation, even if it is as limited as beginning with their own children. In many ways, women discover what has been traditionally known as feminine elements in God: care and concern for children, a defense of life, love, affection, and empathy for suffering. They also encounter a hope for a whole people, a hope that is especially focused on the small and the weak.

This selection of stories is but a representative sample of over one hundred stories I have collected. Certain themes do seem to be relatively constant: the importance of the family, the strength of the mothers despite hardships, the enduring love and faith in Our Lady of Guadalupe, the domestic spirituality and values that are practiced in the home, and the abiding trust in the will of God. The spirituality of these women is lived out not only in their church but in their kitchen, in doing their wash, in their dreams and aspirations, and in the rearing of their children. It is a spirituality that is complex with multiple levels of meaning. Their spirituality entails a meaning that grows over time—and an invitation to deepen the spirituality within ourselves and our self-understanding. As they tell their stories and share their dreams with us we are fortunate to catch a glimpse of the divine at work in their lives. We are challenged to give more women an opportunity to share their spiritual journey, not because we are so different from one another but because our hopes and dreams are so very much the same. The theological enterprise is about giving voice to that hope and doing justice to those dreams.

When the tape recorder is turned off and the women continue to share about their lives, their hopes and their dreams, what emerges is a new consciousness among Latinos. As they increase their ability to articulate their pain, analyze their situation, organize, express their protests and see and commit themselves to radical change for themselves, their children and communities will benefit. This new consciousness has given them the possibility of envisioning ways of being, not just in their personal relationships but in their communities. Women have birthed a new vision which nurtures hope, strength, and extraordinary courage. This inspiring vision is an imaginative leap forward into alternative possibilities and forms of existence born out of the audacity and determination to dream. The metaphor of dreaming, "not in the sense of idle unreality but as a step forward into new realms of existence"[22] is found more than once in the sharing of these U.S. Latina women.

Con carino y amistad—and gratitude to the women who shared their stories—I conclude my reflection.

1. Mercy Amba Oduyoye, "Doing Theology from a Third World Perspective," *Feminist Theology from the Third World: A Reader*, ed. Ursula King (Maryknoll, NY: Orbis Books, 1994), pp. 23–44.

2. Ann Carr, "On Feminist Spirituality," *Women's Spirituality: Resources for Christian Development*, ed. Joann Wolski Conn (New York: Paulist Press, 1986), p. 50.

3. Ivone Gebara, "Women Doing Theology in Latin America," *Feminist Theology from the Third World* (n. 1, above), pp. 47–59.

4. I am indebted to Dr. Roberto Goswaita of Loyola University of Chicago for his insights and challenges to academia regarding this paradigmatic shift in scholarship and his contribution to the paradigmatic that has to happen in theology at the scholar's level. Please see his work "We Are a People."

5. Charles Davis, *The Body as Spirit: The Nature of Religious Feeling* (New York: Seabury Press, 1976), p. 151.

6. Wendy Doniger O'Flaherty, *Other People's Myths* (New York: Macmillan Publishing Co., 1988), p. 27.

7. Eric R. Wolf, "The Virgin of Guadalupe: A Mexican National Symbol," *Journal of American Folklore* 71, 1958, pp. 34–49.

8. Johannes Baptist Metz, *Faith in History and*

Society: Toward a Practical, Fundamental
Theology (New York: Crossroad, 1980), p. 184.

9. *Ibid.*

10. *Ibid.*

11. *Ibid.*

12. *Ibid.*, p. 200.

13. Marcus J. Borg, *Meeting Jesus Again for the First Time* (HarperSanFrancisco, 1995).

14. *Ibid.*, p. 76.

15. Jerome Frank, *Persuasion and Healing* (New York: Schocken Books, 1973), p. 6.

16. Virgilio P. Elizondo, *Galilean Journey: The Mexican-American Promise* (Maryknoll, NY: Orbis Books, 1983).

17. Gloria Anzaldúa, *Borderlands* (San Francisco, Aunt Lute Foundation Books, 1987), pp. 78–81.

18. Gloria Anzaldúa, "La Conciencia de la Mestiza: Towards a New Consciousness," *Making Face, Making Soul*, ed. Gloria Anzaldúa (San Francisco, Aunt Lute Foundation Books, 1990), p. 179.

19. Paula Gunn Allen, *Grandmothers of the Light: A Medicine Woman's Sourcebook* (Boston: Beacon Press, 1991), pp. 5, 6.

20. Donald L. Gelpi, S.J., *Experiencing God: A Theology of Human Emergence* (New York: Paulist Press, 1978), p. 381.

21. Mary Catherine Kilkert, "Experience and Tradition: Can the Center Hold?" *Freeing Theology:*

The Essentials of Theology and Feminist Perspective, ed. Catherine Mowry LaCugna (HarperSanFrancisco: 1993), p. 60.

22. Ursula King, ed., *Feminist Theology from the Third World: A Reader*, (Maryknoll, NY: Orbis Books, 1994).

Selected Bibliography

Paula Gunn Allen. *Grandmothers of the Light*. (Boston: Beacon Press, 1991).

William J. Bausch. *Storytelling: Imagination and Faith*. (Mystic, CT: Twenty Third Publications, 1984).

Marcus J. Borg. *Meeting Jesus Again for the First Time*. (HarperSanFrancisco, 1995).

Charles Davis. *The Body as Spirit: The Nature of Religious Feeling*. (New York: Seabury Press, 1976).

Virgilio P. Elizondo. *Galilean Journey: The Mexican-American Promise*. (Maryknoll, NY: Orbis Books, 1953).

————. *La Morenita: Evangelizer of the Americas*. (San Antonio: Mexican-American Cultural Center, 1980).

Jerome Frank. *Persuasion and Healing*. (New York: Schocken Books, 1973).

Ivone Gebara. "Women Doing Theology in Latin

America." *Feminist Theology from the Third World* (1994).

Guadalupe Gibson. "Hispanic Women: Stress and Mental Health Issues." *Women Changing Therapy*, ed. Joan H. Robbins and R.J. Siegel. (New York: Hayworth Press, 1983).

Mary Catherine Kilkert. "Experience and Tradition: Can the Center Hold?" *Freeing Theology: The Essentials of Theology in Feminist Perspective*, ed. Catherine Mowry LaCugna. (HarperSanFrancisco, 1993).

Johannes Baptist Metz. *Faith in History and Society: Toward a Practical Fundamental Theology.* (New York: Crossroad, 1980).

Mercy Amba Odyyoye. "Doing Theology from a Third World Perspective," *Feminist Theology from the Third World: A Reader*, ed. Ursula King. (Maryknoll, NY: Orbis Books, 1994).

Wendy Doniger O'Flaherty. *Other People's Myths.* (New York: Macmillan Publishing Co., 1988).

Jeanette Rodriguez. "God Is Always Pregnant," *The Divine Mosaic: Women's Images of the Sacred Other*, ed. Theresa King. (St. Paul: Yes International, 1994).

————.*Our Lady of Guadalupe.* (Austin: University of Texas Press, 1994).

Eric R. Wolf. "The Virgin of Guadalupe: A Mexican National Symbol." *Journal of American Folklore* 71 (1958). Also in Livie I. Duran and H. J. Russell

Bernbard, eds. *Introduction to Chicano Studies: A Reader.* (New York: Macmillan Publishing Co., 1973).

Sherna Berger Cluck and Daphne Patai, eds. *Women's Words: The Feminist Practice of Oral History.* (New York: Routledge, 1991).

Adelaila Del Castillo. ed. *Between Borders: Essays on Mexican/Chicana History.* (Encino, CA: Floricanto Press, 1990).

Catherine Mowry LaCugna, ed. *Freeing Theology: The Essentials of Theology in Feminist Perspective.* (HarperSanFrancisco, 1993).

Joann Wolski Conn, ed. *Women's Spirituality: Resources for Christian Development.* (New York: Paulist Press, 1986).

The Madeleva Lecture in Spirituality

This series, sponsored by the Center for Spirituality, Saint Mary's College, Notre Dame, Indiana, honors annually the woman who as president of the college inaugurated its pioneering graduate program in theology, Sister M. Madeleva, C.S.C.

1985
Monika K. Hellwig
Christian Women in a Troubled World

1986
Sandra M. Schneiders
Women and the Word

1987
Mary Collins
Women at Prayer

1988
Maria Harris
Women and Teaching

1989
Elizabeth Dreyer
Passionate Women: Two Medieval Mystics

1990
Joan Chittister
Job's Daughters

1991
Dolores R. Leckey
Women and Creativity

1992
Lisa Sowle Cahill
Women and Sexuality

1993
Elizabeth A. Johnson
Women, Earth and Creator Spirit

1994
Gail Porter Mandell
Madeleva: One Woman's Life

1995
Diana L. Hayes
Hagar's Daughters